THERE IS

HOPE

THE A-Z SURVIVAL GUIDE FOR LIFE'S SITUATIONS

DR. TRACI L. GARDNER-PETTEWAY

There Is Hope: The A-Z Survival Guide for Life's Situations

by Dr. Traci L. Gardner-Petteway

Trade casebound ISBN: 978-1-943294-33-6
Ebook ISBN: 978-1-943294-34-3

Cover design by Martijn van Tilborgh

There Is Hope is also available on Amazon Kindle, Barnes & Noble Nook and Apple iBooks.

CONTENTS

DEDICATION

T HIS BOOK IS FIRST dedicated to "My" Lord and Savior, Jesus, the Christ. I thank you God for your grace and your mercy. I'm living this moment "only" because of you! Second, I would like to thank my husband, Leroy D. Petteway, Jr., for your love, patience, and push (when I wanted to give up). Third, my children: Kendall and Kennedi Grace Petteway; mommy loves you to the moon and back. You both have made my life beautiful and I cannot wait to see what God has for you! My parents, George and Eula Gardner, you both gave me the best life: I grew up in a God-fearing home, attended the best schools, and never needed or wanted for anything! Together you both instilled morals, values, and determination in me and I am forever grateful. My one and only sibling (my big brother) Minister Sheldon George Gardner (retired US Army), I am so proud to tell the world that I am your little sister! You will never know how much I love you!

I have one (1) "female" best friend, Sara Mosley-James! I love you sis and I thank God for our friendship. You are irreplaceable. God gave you to me because He knew "exactly" what I needed (a God-fearing, no-nonsense, tell you like it is…big sis). Wish we weren't three (3)hours away from one another; but I know that you are only one (1) phone call away, a one-way 45-minute flight away, or a 178-mile drive away. I also have one (1) "male" best friend, Dr. Wafeeq Sabir (retired Fort Worth, TX. Gang Intervention and Prevention Police Officer)! As-Salaam-Alaikum my dear friend! Talk about ride or die! We enrolled and earned our Master's Degree (M.A.) together from the "same university" and graduated the "same year", we both married our spouses the "same year", we both became parents the "same year"— both times, and we enrolled and earned our Doctorate of Philosophy (Ph.D.) degrees from the "same university", but he graduated one year ahead of me (he was always the smarter one!). Now, we are both college professors at the "same university" (the University of Phoenix Dallas/ Ft. Worth, Texas, campuses). Wafeeq, you have always been a listening "non-judgmental" ear, you "go off" on me when I began to "cower down" behind madness that's beneath me, you give me a different perspective on controversial topics, and you stand with me and encourage me when all hell has broken loose. Thank you for standing the test of time and being a loyal friend. I can hear you saying to me "Wa-Alaikum-As-Salaam".

God has given me a great circle and I do not take it for granted. I am so blessed.

CHAPTER 1

"A" ADULTERY

ADULTERY IS A TERM that society has tried to "soften." These days it's called an "affair." Adultery is when a man and/or woman, who are joined in Holy matrimony, have sex with another person. An affair is a sexual relationship between "two" people without the other spouse knowing. Both are relationships, but one has a spiritual connotation whereas the other does not "sound" as bad. One has Biblical and Godly principles, whereas the other is socially and politically acceptable.

Regardless of which term you choose to use, when you stand before God and family and make a covenant to "forsake all others," that means regardless of the situation, this particular gift belongs only to that "one" person, your spouse. Just as marriage is sacred to God, sex is sacred to your Christian marriage. This is why God instructs us in the Book of Proverbs, 3rd chapter, 5–6th verses, "… lean not to your own understandings and to acknowledge Him." When we lean, we learn a lesson that can affect the lives of innocent bystanders such as children, parents, and new believers. Proverbs 6 clearly states, "Keeping you from your neighbor's wife, from the smooth talk of a wayward woman"... (vs 24). "Do not lust in your heart after her beauty or let her captivate you with her eyes"… (vs 25).

When we acknowledge Him we become aware of His purpose and His will. God knows we are not perfect, but that's not an excuse to live purposely imperfect lives. Yes, God's a forgiving God, but that is not to be taken for granted. The Bible tells us, "Be not deceived, God cannot be mocked, whatever a man sows is what he will reap" (Galatians 6:7). In other words, you can choose your sin but not your consequences! You may ask, "How do I resist the temptation to commit adultery?" My response is, "YOU PRAY!" You are not blinded by the enemy's devices, and he does not tempt you with anything that is not common/ familiar to you! You will see it coming, so now is not the time to be in denial. As a marriage counselor, I hear it and have heard it all:

1. He says things my husband never says to me;

2. She notices things that my wife never notices;

3. It started out as a simple lunch date; and

4. We work together and one thing led to another.... Really?!?!

The list is socially acceptable excuses and justifications; but with God, there are NO EXCUSES and NO JUSTIFICATIONS!

Satan is slick. "He is walking in and out of the earth" (Job 1:7) seeking whomever he can devour, and he has no shame. He stood before God and told him exactly what he was doing. It wasn't hearsay or secondhand information—it came from the "horse's mouth." Listen to me.... Satan heard the disagreement at home with your spouse and disguised himself as the person who "says everything your spouse does not say." Satan saw you get those expensive highlights in your hair and made sure your husband was distracted when you walked by and didn't notice; then Satan became the man at work who noticed! A man who commits adultery has no sense; whoever does so destroys himself. "Blows and disgrace are his lot, and his shame will ne'er be wiped away" (Proverbs 6:32–33). Lunch dates become dinner dates! Dinner should be at home unless the whole family is out on a dinner date at a restaurant.

CHAPTER 2

"B" BEAUTY

BEAUTY IS IN THE eye of the beholder! I'm sure all of you have heard this infamous quote! There is truth in this statement; however, we must understand that we all have different "truths" based on how and where we were raised! Culture and environment have influence on our perceptions. When I was a young girl growing up in Shreveport, Louisiana, my mother would say very often, when I fell witness to and/or a victim of attractive yet mean girls, "You can be ever so pretty but have ugly ways, and you are ugly."

Society has conditioned many to adopt the media's definition of beauty. Help me understand:

1. When do definitions change?

2. Is there a rationale provided that supports the change?

3. Is or was there a vote?

If beauty is a matter of the heart, and everything that lives has a heart (pretty much), and there are billions of people on this earth, who gets to decide what's beautiful and what's not? There is only one consistency I know and that is God!! Everything He created was and is beautiful—even those creations that have disappointed Him, and He had to rid the earth of them via a flood. 1st Peter 3:3-4 reads, "Your beauty should not come from outward adornment, such as elaborate hairstyles and the wearing of gold jewelry or fine clothes. Rather, it should be that of your inner self, the unfading beauty of a gentle and quiet spirit, which is of great worth in God's sight." No one on this earth should be given that much power over you to convince "you," a creation of God, that you are not beautiful. Line up with and understand God's definition of beauty and you will know, for certain, that you are fearfully and wonderfully made (Psalm 139:14) and that makes you beautiful.

CHAPTER 3

"C" CONDEMNED

"THEREFORE, THERE IS NOW no condemnation for those who are in Christ Jesus" Romans 8:1. That's good news so praise Him for that. There's nothing worse than being the recipient of strong disapproval. It's a pain that cannot be explained. People can say all day, "So what if they don't approve or accept you...." But if you don't understand life through the Spirit of God and walk in it, those who demonstrate disapproval of you will win.

Aren't you tired of people having victory over you? Often people who disapprove of you have issues with themselves as well as issues with accepting themselves for who they are and for who they are not ... think about it! They will never admit it, but they see areas in your life that are obvious favors of the Lord, and to make themselves feel better about their "lack of," they show "disapproval of" you. Isn't it ironic??!! It took me 40 years to grasp that concept and understand where the hate was coming from and, yes, I'm over the age of 40! So much time was wasted focusing on who disapproved and why, and less time focusing on whose approval I should be seeking and who has set me free from condemnation.

Now, don't misunderstand, condemnation and consequences are different. Consequences are the result of actions—good, bad, or indifferent. Condemnation, however, is (based on our discussion) suffering through the disapproval of others, internalizing negative and untruthful opinions, and accepting them as facts. God's approval is paramount in this equation. Remember, people have no heaven or hell to place you in. Now, they may give you hell while on earth, but they may be catching hell as well because of their own self-inflicted wounds. One thing I know for certain—the ones who disapprove of you are not mentioned in the Book of Revelations as "worthy" to open the Book of Life; they can't even write their name, let alone someone else's name, in the Book of Life. So what does that tell you? #NONFACTOR!

CHAPTER 4

"D" DOMESTIC VIOLENCE

THIS IS DEFINITELY A growing epidemic in our society. People believe they have the authority to exert their will over another person. There are two incidences that bothered my spirit and postulated a double standard, in my professional opinion:

1. The incident between rapper Mogul Jay Z and his sister-in-law, Solange, and

2. The incident between professional athlete Ray Rice and his then fiancée, Janay.

Some women were *cheering Solange* and *dejecting Ray Rice*. Isn't that a double standard? Violence is wrong—period. No one has the right to hit another person, *REGARDLESS*. Women and men are to restrain themselves. Men and women are not to provoke one another.

In most cases, domestic violence is an environmental issue and is viewed as a generational curse. We fail to realize the impact and influence "exposure" has during childhood. Albert Bandura coined the Social Learning Theory that simply states that children learn through observation. Now please do not run off on the left side—stay with me! Violence can also be observed outside of the home, on television, at a neighbor's house, or even on a video game. I'm talking about what "you" see or "have seen" while you were growing up—good, bad, or indifferent—and how your life may or may not have been impacted as a result of it.

In some cases, violence in the home was the norm, and in other cases, violence in the home is the new norm! Whatever it took for a person to get their way or exert power over another person, that was the method of choice. Please don't overlook the word "choice." You do have a choice!

When you want to push—pray.

When you want to punch—pray.

When you disagree—listen to know what to pray for

If you want to understand—listen with the intent to understand.

CHAPTER 5

"E" EDUCATION

"THE ELEVATOR TO SUCCESS is broken ... you must take the stairs." This is a quote that my former professor/dean, the late Dr. Joseph Capers, shared with me during my undergraduate years at Wiley College in Marshall, Texas. He actually spoke these words to me during my coronation! Yes, I'm a Historically Black College "Queen"! Every year the course work became more challenging. The curriculum was developed that way ... to enhance learning, develop critical thinking skills, and create an awareness of proper application! Although he was referencing "college" education, the quote still reigns in self-awareness. Every year you should learn something about yourself to improve upon as well as to eliminate, because it is toxic to you and others.

Just as you invest time and work into excelling academically in college, to be promoted (or become promotable at work) you must invest time and work in YOU personally, as well as your significant other selection process. You have what you tolerate and you teach people how to treat and how to talk to you. Educate yourself on that person you are giving your best time and effort to! There may be some crucial past events and circumstances that you "need to know" and not find out on an "as you go" basis. There is a difference, and the difference can be life changing. "Need to know" are such things as religious beliefs, family values, personal and professional goals! An "as you go" basis is "after the fact." For example, you become aware that the person you are with is a registered sex offender and can't be around children—theirs or yours. You may say, "That's a little extreme," but trust me, this happens more often than you realize.

It wasn't disclosed, of course, until you invited them to a family reunion or event and they declined and you asked them why. Let's say it together ... "awkward." That person knew the information entering into the relationship, but they withheld that information ... so now the questions on the table are ... "What else haven't you told me?" or "What else do I need to know?" Educate yourselves.

CHAPTER 6

"F" FORNICATION

THIS IS A SINGLE person having sex with another single and/or married person. A single person cannot commit adultery; married people commit adultery. Here is yet another term that is sexual in content that society has changed to make socially acceptable ... the Bible calls it "fornication" ... society refers to it as "dating"... wow, that new word certainly sounds better, huh??!!

Where I'm from, and many of you "my age and older" will agree, dating was going to a movie, dinner, or a concert. Sex is sex. When meanings change, the act tends to become more acceptable ... the "new normal." Call it what it is. In the call, there is conviction, and where there is secrecy, there is sin.

Fornication, for the sake and purposes of this chapter, is consensual, but the term carries an overtone of moral and religious disapproval. The Greek word for fornication is "porneia," which is where the term pornography comes from. 1 Corinthians 6:18–20 provides principles for marriage: "... Two become one flesh, one spirit, free from sexual immorality." It is good for a "man" to not have sexual relations with a "woman" (if not married), but because of the temptation (lack of self-control) to sexual immorality, each man should have his own "wife" and each woman her own "husband"—in other words, get married.

Sexual immorality is a sin that has consequences, just as all sin does. Remember, you cannot choose the consequences of the sin you commit knowingly and/or unknowingly. Choose your actions wisely for they can have a "not so pleasant" eternal and earthly impact, as well as cause families (innocent bystanders) unnecessary battle scars.

CHAPTER 7

"G" GOSSIP

THE BIBLE SPEAKS TO every possible life situation you can think of. For example, in 1 Timothy 5:13, Paul says "they learn (**not born that way**) to be idlers," (**not enough of their own things to deal with**) "going from house to house, and not only idlers, but also gossips and busybodies, saying what they should not." Things people should talk about they do not. Gossip is idle talk and/or rumors, especially about the personal or private affairs of others. Biblically, gossip is wrong; but socially, gossip is entertainment (here we go again changing the definition of words to make them socially acceptable). That which is used specifically to spread dirt and misinformation is exciting. This is an unhealthy but widely practiced behavior that leads to destruction—destruction of the gossiper and the victim. Allow me to provide you some suggestions that I commonly refer to as the "Four R's" of gossip:

1. **R**ise above the gossip.

2. **R**ealize what/who caused it or fueled it.

3. **R**efuse to participate.

4. **R**ebuke it so it will go away from you and them.

You may remember that I've mentioned that you teach people how to treat you! Well, if you entertained gossip once, you will continue to be entertained by gossip because you opened the door as a listening ear. If you stop the messenger/carrier of the gossip before they start, they will know that you are not one to listen and they will not bring it to you. Many times the messenger does not know if the message is true or not! The story is a hot topic and they choose to "gossip" about it.

CHAPTER 8

"H" HOSTILE WORK ENVIRONMENT

A HOSTILE WORK ENVIRONMENT IS one in which there is discrimination and harassment of employees based on a variety of reasons. Unfortunately, women experience this more often than men. The question on the table is, "Which is the hardest to deal with—reporting it or dealing with it?" The hardest, in my professional opinion and based on information I've been made privy to, is reporting, because women do not receive the emotional and psychological support that's needed once the whistle has been blown. There was a middle-aged woman who experienced, and suffered through, a hostile working environment, and it became hostile when she refused to succumb to the sexual advances of her immediate supervisor.

Her refusing to fulfill his sexual fantasy led to him refusing to sign off on her hours worked, refusing to pay her the agreed upon salary, and telling her that her 90-day probationary period was going to be very hard for her. He was right—it was brutal.

However, the "aftermath" was even worse. She informed the appropriate people (the Board of Directors, who were all men) and initially, when they approached her supervisor, he (of course) denied it; but once they made him privy to strong self-incriminating evidence, he ADMITTED to ALL OF IT—every single bit—and resigned. He did not leave quietly. He's always been a loose cannon. Even though a gag order was issued and put into place for him and the Board of Directors (again, all men), they all talked—actually, just as much as the women. "Distortion" was spread by the gossiper(s) and left to the imagination of the "ears" they were speaking into.

The hardest and most humbling part for her was dealing with the people—mostly women ... yes, ... the women. She could not wrap her brain around the looks, the comments, and being ostracized.... she said, "No," but was treated and handled as if she said "Yes." She was not the only one. There were more than 20 others and under-aged children, but since "she" spoke up, she became the scapegoat.

This incident enlightened me to fully understand and realize why victims of rape do not report the incident. It's not only the perpetrator of the rape (i.e., the villain) who they are fearful of; it's also the other people who were not involved, who weren't there, who listened to the gossipers, who don't know the facts of the matter, and the villain's ride or die family and/or friends.

My dear sisters, you have the right to love your career and get paid for the work you provide without being told that you have to fulfill short or long-term sexual fantasies of a mentally disturbed, sexually perverted, supervisor. Trust me, you are not the first and you will not be the last, unless you take a stand and report it. You may have to stand alone with Jesus, but that's OK.... He will carry you!

I cannot explain how "alone" the feeling of "standing alone" was for her. Interestingly enough, after the exposure of inappropriate conduct, numerous victims came forward; (husbands, wives, and children who are now young adults) but only her name remained on the hot topics list as the villain and not the victim. Not sure how that happened, but it did. Nevertheless, God knows, and He kept her mind sane, her health perfect, and her focus on Him. That's how she survived; and you can, too! Does it hurt? Yes, it hurt her like hell. The truth "made her free," and she "now" sleeps peacefully at night; but now "I" pray for other victims, who felt they had to, or currently have to, succumb to unwanted sexual advances to keep their jobs and who are now prisoners at work.

CHAPTER 9

"I" IN-LAWS

GOD'S PLAN FOR MARRIAGE focuses on leaving the "dependence" on your parents and "cleaving" to your spouse. Dependence can be emotional, financial, or both. In the Old Testament "God" says in Genesis 2:24 that a "... man shall leave his father and his mother and cleave to his wife." In the New Testament, Jesus said that no one was ever intended to come between husband and a wife (Matthew 19:6). No in-laws, outlaws, no mother, and no father was meant to divide a couple who had made a covenant with each other to leave, cleave, and become one flesh.

One thing I know for certain is that shifting loyalty from parent to spouse is hard, but if you don't, marital conflict will be inevitable. I'm a daddy's girl, and I've been one "ALL MY LIFE." I love my mother, so don't run off to Louisiana or call her saying otherwise. :-) The hardest thing for me was not running to my dad with my hurts and pain because ... "I have a husband." Not that my husband was not capable—we are just creatures of habit! Leaving and cleaving does not mean permanently withdrawing, because the Book of Exodus 20:12 is the 1st Commandment with a Promise! Honor your parents (love and respect) so that your days may be long on this earth.

OK, now the "flipside"—parents must let go, too! Momma's boy is now another woman's MAN! Daddy's girl is now another man's WOMAN! Everyone must accept and operate in their "God Ordained" role. If not, you (the parents) will find yourselves the "cause" of your "married child" experiencing and suffering through a divorce—sad, depressed, seeing their child/children every other weekend and alternating holidays, and the *RISK* of the ex-wife/ex-husband meeting and starting a new relationship. Sounds tough doesn't it??!! There's more—that new relationship can lead to re-marriage, and now that new "step-parent" is playing an active role in raising, nurturing, disciplining, and developing the child/children. And they have every right, within the court of law, to do so. So new married couples—leave and cleave. In-laws—mind the matters of your household; be a help and support to that new family!

CHAPTER 10

"J" JEALOUSY

I N T H E 1 9 8 0 ' S T H E R E was an R&B group called Club Nouveau and they had a song titled "Jealousy." Pretty cool song, nice beat, and at the time, I was just singing the words! As I look back and reflect, the words were powerful! Jealousy is an emotion that encompasses feelings of fear, then rage and humiliation, then insecurity and anxiety. Men and women can experience jealousy when they feel that a third party could possibly threaten their relationship. In this life, you will experience some form of jealousy, but you must remember that we defined jealousy as a form of insecurity; it is much healthier to acknowledge your insecurities, understand the "root" cause, and then find methods of dealing with it in a productive manner. Nothing good comes from jealousy. Galatians 5:20: "... jealousy..." verse 21 "...

and envy ..." will not inherit the kingdom of God. There is no room.

We are visual individuals, and we see things and admire people not realizing that we only see the surface—the finished, or should I say, the polished product. It reminds me of Sigmund Freud's "Psycho-Analytic Theory," which is often referred to visually as an iceberg; you see the tip (that which is above water), but it's what's beneath the water that could change a good day into a "not-so-good" day. We don't see the pain, sweat, tears, etc. during the process. We look at others and wish and wonder, not knowing what they lost in the name of trying to make it. Everyone has sacrificed (i.e., lost) something in pursuit of something.

Hebrews 13:5 instructs us to be content with what we have. What God has for "you" is for "you," and there is nothing anyone else can do but influence you to think you can't have it. This is what keeps you in bondage to envy and jealousy—envious and jealous people. Separate yourself from that "stinkin' thinkin'" mentality before it consumes you. The secret to being content is located in Philippians 4:12: "Trust God." You cannot trust if you have a spirit of jealousy.

CHAPTER 11

"K" KINFOLK

YOU CANNOT CHOOSE THE family that you are born into, but you do have "some" input on the family you marry into! This is why it is important to date and get to know your prospective spouse and their family. Take your time! It is also equally important that you allow your "person of interest" to get to know your family. Now, please realize that just because you introduce everyone to one another does not mean that everyone will be accepting, loving, and kind. Not only must you realize this, but you must also be "OK" with it.

Not everyone in your family is going to love the person you love! However, respect is expected and you have what you tolerate! I know many of you would love to have the fairytale book "happily ever after" and the "can't we all get along" syndrome, we all do. But the reality is, this is not a perfect world, and the Bible tells us in James 1:2, "Count it all joy when you meet trials of various kinds," and 1 Peter 1:6, "In this you rejoice, though now for a little while, if necessary, you have been grieved by various trials."

You will experience and have to endure hardships, hurt, and pain as a result of dealing with "your kinfolk." Does it hurt? Of course it does. It's different when non-family members cause hardships, hurt, and pain versus family members. We have higher levels of expectations for our family members. There will be times that both "kinfolk" and "non-kinfolk" will "bring the pain," but remember 1 Corinthians 14:33: "For God is not of confusion but of peace." Since we know that Satan is the author of confusion, you have to "Pray the hell out of them" so that you can operate in Romans 12:18: "… live peaceably with all." You have to spend time with his/her immediate family! You are not "technically" marrying the aunts, uncles, cousins, etc., but you may have to interact with some of them from time to time, and "people and relationships perish due to a lack of knowledge"! There will be times that some "kinfolk" are just hard to deal with for various reasons.

Another situation, in which I have been made privy of, parallels to the message I'm trying to convey. There was a couple who had a great "dating" relationship. He was an only child and he had been married previously. So, she was unfortunately subjected to scrutiny from his mother and ridicule from his friends because no one was good enough for him. Everything was an issue and peace just would not be still. It was as if she, and his mother, were fighting over a man that they both wanted (sounds funny doesn't it)!! Even though they both had a rightful place in his life and a "God Ordained" role to operate in ... it was a problem. The first few years of their marriage was extremely challenging, everything BUT bliss, to say the least. There were many days, weeks, and months that she mentioned, "I'm still young, I look good {smile}, and I can do this thing over again with someone else with fewer battle scars." Her husband's father, aunts, uncles, and cousins were very loving and encouraging, and "some" friends were very accepting, but some of those "friends" created temporary and minimal roadblocks, too! Thanks to almighty God for deliverance and time, she was able to look at and around those nouns (people/roadblocks) and see those "storm chasers" for who they really were—people with major issues of their own.

When you marry, you are joining forces with one other person (opposite sex) and uniting as one with the one and only true God. External relationships are great to have and they can be fulfilling (most of the time); however, the most important relationship is not with "external factors" but with the "internal factor" who provides "eternal benefits."

CHAPTER 12

"L" LOVE

Love is a word that is used loosely these days, but one that has changed the world. For God so "loved" the world that He gave His only begotten son! (John 3:16a). I heard someone say, "God has some hard rules!" I responded, "Why do you say that?" The answer was, "Everyone that God tells me to love is not lovable!" I smiled and asked a simple question: "Are you lovable all the time?" Silence filled the room. No one is lovable all the time, but you must love and love on credit!

If you are honest with yourself and others, you know that you are not 100% lovable on even your best day! So why do you have high requirements and expectations of others when you don't meet the mark yourself? This may sound harsh to some, but the truth hurts sometimes. Realizing and accepting the truth is where the healing and growth begins. Real love is unconditional, and it sees past the faults in others. Many individuals schedule appointments with me, and the most popular statement I hear is "I thought they loved me." The question I generally ask is: "Why do you feel that they didn't?"

We define love based on what we have experienced, how we act/show love, and what we have been taught. The definition may vary from person to person, culture to culture. You must use the love of God as the standard (i.e., measuring stick). You can use God's love as the standard once you truly understand and know what God's love is. There are four (4) steps I recommend for knowing what God's love is: (1) **R**ead His word, (2) **S**tudy His word, (3) **P**ray His word, and (4) **W**ait for Him (Isaiah 40:31). My church's Minister of Music, Dr. Patrick D. Bradley, taught the Westside Baptist Church Mass Choir a praise and worship song years ago titled "I Will Give You the Praise," and the words are simple and true: "For to know Him is to love Him, and to love Him is to serve Him." You will not know, experience, or give love effectively until you know and understand God's love, because He is love. He loves us in spite of ourselves.

Nothing we are supposed to do is easy. It's easy to love those who are lovable or who love you back; it's the one who is unlovable and who shows no love at all that's the challenge. One thing I tell couples often is that you may not "like" your spouse today, but you should "love" them today. There will be days that you will not agree, but you shouldn't lose love. If that were the case ... God would have stopped loving us a long time ago! I hear couples say often in my office, "relationships are 50/50"; I immediately correct them by responding, "No, relationships are 100/100." You give 100 and your spouse gives 100. Now, there will be days when you may fall short on your end ... maybe you're averaging 85% today. Guess what? Now your spouse has to love you on credit (115%) until you get it together.

CHAPTER 13

"M" MARRIAGE

MARRIAGE IS THE UNION between man and woman, which is now one of the most controversial topics in the world. However, the beauty of this book is that I'm the author and I operate and submit to Joshua 24:15: "... as for me and my house we will serve the Lord." Likewise, as a Christian who believes the entire Bible, I stand on 2 Timothy 3:16–17: "All scripture is breathed out by God and profitable for teaching, for reproof, for correction, and for training in righteousness, that the man of God may be complete, equipped for every good work." So with all that being said, marriage is between man and woman.

Marriage is work. Just as you may apply for employment and the job requirements are provided, there are also "other duties as assigned"!

Well, in a marriage you have two people coming together as one. Two people, including all of their past hurts, pains, accomplishments, disappointments, etc. So, in marriage, there is a disclaimer that simply means—it is not going to be easy but it's worth it, if you marry for the right reasons. I have noticed in my profession that people marry for many different reasons, but when a problem arises, they can't seem to remember what the "real" or "deal breaking" reason was.

A major and life-lasting reason is "unconditional" love. Galatians 5:22 makes it clear what the fruit of the spirit is: love, joy, peace, patience, kindness, goodness, and self-control. If you don't have these characteristics as a "single person," the likelihood of you being capable of earnestly demonstrating these traits are slim to none. I am not saying that you must "master" these characteristics, but they should be a goal that you are striving toward—not working against. Marriage must have a "living foundation," which means that the "one true and living God" must be the center—the core—of your relationship. No exceptions! Once you understand the "Love of God" and "His" ordination of marriage, you are able to understand your role in the marriage that He has ordained. Marriage should not be rushed "into" out of convenience or "financial sense," and it shouldn't be rushed "out of" as a result of a disagreement or temporary life situations or circumstances. Just as you have to incorporate problem-solving skills at work, you must do the same in a marriage.

The problem-solving guide that has the best practices is the Holy Bible. Matthew 19 vs 6b: "What therefore God has joined together, let no man separate." Marriage is sacred. Marriage is ordained by God, and He has put into place guidelines to follow that will sustain your marriage—the Holy Bible. I strongly recommend pre-marital counseling because there are some topics that "excited couples" do not talk about (or forget to talk about) that should be discussed, such as finances, "in-laws," friends, church membership, etc. The topics mentioned are also situations that can lead to disagreements and the demise of a marriage.

Since God proclaims marriage, there is someone who despises marriage—Satan. Sometimes we make Satan's job easy. Satan is associated with sin and Jesus is associated with salvation. Sin entered marriage with Adam and Eve. Sin will exit when Jesus comes back for His bridegroom … that's us! Marriage is a decision that you choose to progress into. You do not go into it with your eyes closed. Marriage is work … hard work. There will be good days and bad days, and they may not always be in balance. But the foundation of your marriage is what keeps it "in balance."

The foundation is God. When you have the right foundation, you understand 1 Corinthians 13: 7–8b: "Love bears all things, believes all things, hopes all things, endures all things. Love never ends." This society has many different views of marriage; however, God says that marriage is one man *and* one woman. Your spouse should be your confidante, your biggest supporter, your honest critic, your prayer partner, and your friend. You should have things in common with your spouse, and just as you have things you share in common, there will be things you do not have in common. This is where sacrifice steps in. Ladies, if you're not into sports, consider watching a game with him. Men, you may not like shopping, but go to the mall with her. In addition to sacrifices, you need to continue to date one another after you get married. A date night every month can make a world of difference in your marriage. Ladies, remember how you'd dress up, get your manicure and pedicure, schedule an appointment with your hairstylist, etc. because you and your "boyfriend" were going out?? That still needs to happen. Men, remember how you'd plan a special evening, get a fresh haircut, and clean out your car?? That still needs to happen. This is how you keep the excitement and break up the normal routine.

CHAPTER 14

"N" NEGLECT

THERE ARE TIMES WHEN we are so consumed with taking care of others and attending to their needs that we fail to take care of ourselves. Regardless of how you try to say it, when you fail to take care of yourself you are "neglecting" yourself. How beneficial can you possibly be if you are not running efficiently yourself? There are numerous areas in which we neglect ourselves; however, I will discuss the two (2) most common: mentally and spiritually.

Many people do not realize that what we process we project. We have no control over the thoughts that "pop" into our heads, but we do have control over what we "do with" those thoughts and "how long" we meditate on those thoughts. Mental neglect impacts self-esteem, how you treat others, as well as how you view and treat yourself. There are several proven successful ways to counter mental neglect: having powerful mental stimulants, a strong circle of supporters (no enablers allowed), determination, focus, and the removal of toxic people from your inner circle. Everyone does not deserve front row/ priority seating in your life ... the balcony section is available for those individuals.

You also must gain control over what you allow into your hearing, especially since we know (should know) that faith comes by "hearing" (Romans 10:17). It is imperative that you protect your hearing, because what you hear, if you're not careful, becomes your thoughts; and your thoughts have the capacity to influence your objectivity and behavior. Your behavior is a direct signal to what is going on with and inside of you. So, do not neglect yourself mentally.

We also find ourselves neglecting ourselves spiritually. My new pastor, as of May 2015, Rev. Thomas N. Bessix (Westside Baptist Church of Lewisville, Texas), continuously reminds us of the importance of refueling. We enter into His gates with Thanksgiving and into His courts with Praise, but most only enter on Sundays!!!! Most churches have Prayer Meetings, Women and Men's Ministry, and Wednesday Bible Study. These are gospel teaching opportunities that "refuel." I'm not saying that you should "take up" residence at the church, but rather that the church should be in you. But life is hard and this society throws curve balls daily, along with the nouns (people, places, and things) in your life. If you neglect your spiritual nourishment, you will cause your spiritual immune system to weaken, thus resulting in you becoming susceptible to the tricks of the devil. It is also imperative that you read and study the word of God for yourself. Private refueling allows opportunity for you and God to have quality time—refueling.

I have a funny story to tell you! My husband has always cautioned me about allowing the gas to run "too low" in my car. Well, the reserve fuel light came on in my car one night and I just ignored it and said to myself, "I have enough fuel to get home." Even though "my car" warned me more than once that I was low on fuel and asked me if I needed help locating the nearest gas station, I ignored the warning signs. All of a sudden, my car just stopped; I ran out of gas (can you believe that?). No more fuel. And without fuel, my car would not run. I had to contact Triple "A" (AAA Texas) and they had to come out and give me fuel on the side of the road. I didn't realize how fast the cars were going in traffic until I was sitting still. Are you that way? You see the warning signs but do not heed God's voice because you are neglecting yourself spiritually. Or, do you wait until crisis mode before you contact Him? Triple

"A" of Texas (AAA) is always there *when you call*, but "**THE**" Triple "A" never leaves: **A**lpha, **A**lmighty, **A**nchor. God gives us warning signs; the question is: "Are we paying attention?" Don't neglect your spiritual refueling ... your future movement and progression depends on it.

CHAPTER 15

"O" OPPOSITION

MY GRANDMOTHER (the late Mrs. Essie Lee Davis) would often say, "What doesn't kill you will make you strong!" OMG (Oh My Goodness). I truly thought that some situations I found myself "fighting through" were going to place the nail in my coffin, but I made it through. Opposition is simply defined as resistance that is typically expressed in an action and/or argument. In this life you will encounter various trials (i.e., opposition); but, it's not what happens to you ... it's how you handle it. You can <u>allow it</u> to deal with you and destroy everything you've worked for, or you can deal with it before it destroys everything you've worked for. So, you may be asking yourself, how do I deal with opposition? Well, great question, and I will gladly answer!

First, you must *understand the source* of the opposition. This may be difficult because it could be coming from various directions. Once you identify the source (usually a person), you must secondly *"stop" and "consider"* the role <u>you</u> "may have" played in the opposition. This is tough to do because it requires a self-evaluation! You will discover one of two things...1) you are suffering from self-inflicted wounds, or 2) you are on the receiving end through no fault of your own. Either one is humbling. Let's discuss both scenarios!

If you are receiving opposition as a result of *self-inflicted wounds*, pray first and thank God for the revelation, because <u>many people</u> do not see the harvest of the seed "they" planted, and denial sets in! An example of "denial sets in" is simply this statement: "It's not me, it's them." After the prayer of thanks, ask God to give you the right words to say to the "source" and ask God to prepare and open the heart and mind of the "source" to receive your words. Now, I need to tell you something ... please realize that "people are people" and this is a very unforgiving, blaming and grudge-holding society. The source may know the right thing to do and they may "see" your sincerity, but that does not mean they will do the right thing. When this happens, and you've done your part ... refer to Matthew 10:14: "If anyone will not receive you or listen to your words, shake off the dust from your feet when you leave...." It's so amazing to know that there is nothing in this world that God does not address and provide guidance for through His Holy Word. Now, on the flipside, if they are forgiving and receptive, acknowledge how you contributed to the opposition, offer resolution, AND ask them for their thoughts about resolution, too.

If you are experiencing opposition, through no fault of your own, understand that people (i.e. haters) will bring problems to your front door. As I have mentioned earlier in this book, jealousy will cause people to do and say some horrible things. Jealousy is an outward demonstration of low self-esteem and many other lows. People with low self-esteem will gladly bring opposition into your life. You could have a great idea, a great presence, education, poise, the respect of your peers ... just the favor of God ... and they <u>hate you</u> for it. They have no idea the *prayers you've prayed*, how many *tears you've cried,* the *sacrifices made* ... they can't see your *battle scars* ... all they see is the aftermath. I will share with you what my father has embedded in my spirit because I have fallen victim to self-inflicted opposition as well as no-fault opposition. When you have fallen victim to "no-fault" opposition, as my daddy would say to me: "Sweetheart, you cannot be over-concerned for under-concerned people." Pray daily asking God to help you understand and accept Ecclesiastes 1:15: "... there are people who are crooked and will not be made straight ..." because God has, according to Romans 1:28: "... turned them over to a reprobate mind." It's a hopeless cause, and the wrestle is not flesh and blood ... it's spiritual warfare. Can't fight spiritual warfare without the Spirit of God dwelling inside of you.

Opposition is not fun whether it is self-inflicted or no fault of your own. But you must deal with it on your knees because you will need strength to stand up and endure. Move from your knees to your feet and walk in faith. As you walk in faith, you must speak and deal with the "source" in love!

CHAPTER 16

"P" PARENTING

THE TOUGHEST JOB YOU will ever love. Parenting is a **privilege**. Parenting requires **patience**. Parents must **persevere**. Parents must **provide**. As a child growing up, I loved playing with dolls. I was always the loving mommy and I'd cook, feed, change their clothes, and comb their hair. One thing I have taught my students in higher learning (i.e., college) is the Social Learning Theory, which was coined by Albert Bandura in 1977. This theory simply states that children learn through observation, and they mimic what they see. So, as a child, the way my mother handled me was the way I handled my dolls. When I became an adult and a mommy, I found myself handling my children the same exact way my mom handled me and my brother. Prayerfully, the saga will continue on through my daughter and son! Not everyone is a parent. Not everyone was or is created to be a parent, just as not every woman is or was created to be a mother. So those women who are blessed with the opportunity to be a mother or to parent should not take it lightly. It is a privilege. I know many couples who have tried all medical technologies to conceive a child without success. Children are the responsibility of their parents or primary caregivers. Yes, it takes a village, but the primary responsibility is the primary parent/caregiver.

Children do not ask to be born, but once those little angels are here, they demand our attention; this means that parenting requires patience. Unfortunately, children are having to grow up fast for various reasons: taking care of younger siblings, babies having babies, etc. Children are children and they love to play and they learn in stages; this is often referred to as the modality of developmental stages. You must exercise patience because children develop and learn at their own pace, and being impatient with them frustrates you, the parent! This demonstrated behavior toward the child (i.e., frustration) causes the child to feel unnecessary disappointment. This disappointment leads to low self-esteem and self-awareness issues.

Parenting is challenging, but we must persevere. Perseverance simply means continuing on the course of action even in the face of difficulty. Life happens, but you must stay the course, especially as a parent, because your children are watching you. Remember, "they learn through observation." One of my favorite books is titled "The Road Less Traveled," written by M. Scott Peck, M.D. (1978). The first three (3) words of his book are life changing: "Life is Hard." This is a very profound statement. Parenting is hard, but we must persevere. When children are born, there is no blueprint. However, we are called to parent to the best of our abilities. We should invest in our children's social well-being, spiritual development, and educational development.

Investing in your child's social well-being implies that you involve your child in activities that are beneficial for social interaction, development, and cultural diversity. As adults, when we pursue employment, we cannot choose our co-workers; so, it's most advantageous that we as parents (or primary caregivers) incorporate activities in our children's lives that will prepare them for where they are headed—being surrounded by other individuals who do not look like them, act like them, etc. The activities do not have to be "high financial obligatory" activities; however, you also need to factor in that you get what you pay for, so choose wisely! There are many quality youth programs spread across the communities such as 1) YMCA Sports, 2) local recreation centers, and 3) Boy and Girl Scouts of America. These are cost-effective value-added programs that assist with providing social interaction, development, and definitely cultural diversity.

Perseverance also applies to being active in the school and the school district in which your child is enrolled. Back-to-school night should be just as crowded as Black Friday. Parent/teacher conferences should be just as crowded as the day after Christmas shopping! It is not the sole responsibility of the teacher to educate your child. You "both" have a role. Luke 12:48b makes it very plain, "For unto whomsoever <u>much is given</u>, of him shall be <u>much required</u>..."

CHAPTER 17

"Q" QUALITY

W E H E A R A N D U S E this term quite often, but do we really know what it means? Quality is a measure of excellence, free from defects; but also has consistent commitment to certain standards. Now, we all define words differently, but the root definition should center on "free from defects." Your life should be free from defects! You may be thinking or saying, "I don't have any defects in my life." Well a defect "defined" is the lack of something necessary for completeness. A defect can be a noun in your life (person, place, or thing). What's in your life that you are attaching quality characteristics to that actually has a defective recall?

You must realize and remind yourself that you are fearfully and wonderfully made (Psalm

139:14). That means that quality was placed in you (in all of us), so what's *in* you should radiate *through* you! If you are connected with anything less than what was placed in you, there is a strong possibility that you may be infected with "defectitus" and you will need an antibiotic. The antibiotic will include one (1) hip injection (i.e., butt cheek) of the Holy Spirit and a seven (7)-day prescription of three (3) pills per day: one of the Father, one of the Son, and one of the Holy Spirit, morning, noon and night.

God took His time, meaning that He was in no rush to create or incorporate "quality" in us. That being said, we should take our time and not be in a rush to allow anything in our lives that is not going to enhance what has already been delicately placed in us. Our "quality" of life depends greatly on who/what we allow into our lives; we have what we tolerate.

Many of you may feel that you've had so many defects in your life that you are permanently infected. Let me assure you that once you have removed the defects and moved forward, "You have been set free" (Romans 6:18). When you **"Release," "Remove,"** and **"Renew,"** it will feel like a weight has been lifted. Quality is the standard, and do not settle for anything less.

CHAPTER 18

"R" RESPECT

W HEN I HEAR OR see the word "Respect," the Queen of Soul, Aretha Franklin, pops into my head. "What you want, baby I've got it. What you need, you know I've got it. All I ask is for a little respect ... just a little bit!" LOL! There is so much truth in this song. We all want respect. Some need just a little bit; others need a whole lot! However, due to life's situations and circumstances, we find it hard to respect those who "we deem" unworthy of our respect. So that we are on the same page, let's define respect, or at least give you a working definition for the sake of this publication. Respect is a "feeling" of admiration based on "good qualities" (remember, nothing is good or bad unless it's compared to something, so everyone's view will vary!). Respect is also a "demonstrated behavior" which shows that you are aware of someone's rights.

As a marriage coach, I have met with numerous couples and I have emphasized the importance and the need for women to feel loved and safe in a relationship, as well as the importance and need for men to feel respect in a relationship. When any one of those is missing on either side, there will be a problem. This is not to say that women do not have a need for respect, and vice versa for men. The statement is based on my professional observation of situations presented to me over 15 years of service to the profession.

In a relationship, married or dating (or even parenting), disrespect is not acceptable. You teach people how to talk to you and how to treat you. If you actively participate in a dialogue that is filled with explicit words and derogatory statements "the first time," the saga will continue because you participated and allowed it. When you foresee the conversation transcending from constructive to destructive, that's when you remove yourself and/or refuse to participate. Remember the old adage, "It's not what you say; it's how you say it." Not only will people "try" to talk to you crazy (as we say in Louisiana), but people will also "try" to treat you disrespectfully. Again, you have what you tolerate. If you set the standard during the beginning stages of the relationship and not deviate from it, the happier you will be and the more consistent your relationship will be.

CHAPTER 19

"S" STRENGTH

THINK I AM THE biggest Whitney Houston fan. My favorite song (although I love all of her songs) is titled, "I Didn't Know My Own Strength." We never truly know how strong and resilient we are until the storm comes and goes. We look back and say, "Wow, how did I get through that?" My grandmother taught me her favorite scripture, which was Psalm 121:1: "I will look to the hills from whence comes my help for my help comes from the Lord." So when I would go through things, I would take the scripture she taught me and begin reciting it.

You may not feel, during the storm, that you have any strength, but you are stronger than you think! My mother was also very inspiring, and she would always tell me to make sure that

I do not look like whatever it is that I'm going through. She would say that every single day is a new opportunity to make a difference, so put your best foot forward, put your makeup on before you walk out of the house, comb your hair, dress well, and smile—even when you feel like crying.

There were times I would get tired of hearing her tell me this, but it was the best advice a mother could tell her daughter. There are people who wake up daily longing for you to fail in your personal and professional life. So, since "people are out there just waiting for you to mess up," remember this passage of scripture, which can be found in 1 John 4:4b: "... greater is He who is in you, than he who is in the world."

Then at the end of each and every phone conversation she would close by saying, "Now put your hands in the Lord's hand and I will too, stay focused, and stay positive." Now those words helped me build and maintain my strength! We tend to sometimes operate outwardly based on how we feel inwardly. That has to change. We have to learn and practice operating outwardly based on what we know spiritually. That's how we recognize God's power in our lives and the strength He empowers us with.

I was not built to break and neither were you!

CHAPTER 20

"T" TRUST

GIVEN SO FREELY, LOST so easily! The word of God instructs us to "Trust in the Lord with all thine heart ..." (Proverbs 3:5). We tend to want to place our trust in "ourselves" or in "another person," and that's where we miss the mark every time. There are many perspectives related to what trust is, and due to my extensive background in psychology and sociology, you will get the best of both worlds from me! From a psychological perspective, trust is believing that the other person involved will do what is expected. It starts with the family and grows to others. From a sociological perspective, the role of trust is the major concern.

We expect people to do what they say they are going to do, when they stated they were going to do it, with no excuses or exceptions. We often "forget" that we also commit or overcommit ourselves and sometimes we are not able to deliver. However, when certain people say they are going to do something, the level of expectation increases. There are times when we sincerely commit to helping others, but life happens. In efforts to not disappoint, we try to "make good" on our commitment; sometimes, we just need to admit that we cannot deliver so that adjustments can be made. Trying to do what you cannot may cause more harm than good.

Many people are aware that my husband travels frequently inside and outside of the country. Often I hear comments such as, "Do you trust him?" or "How do you know what he's doing or not doing?" My response is very simple. "I trust God." Once you realize where your trust should be, your life becomes a lot easier. Now, don't misunderstand. I am human and there were times when I allowed the things people "said" to influence my interaction with him. Then I had to realize that when you allow "certain" things into your hearing, you have opened the door for Satan to use those words to create doubt that was never there. I cannot worry about things that I have no control over. Remember the "serenity prayer"? All I can do is continue to be the "woman of God" that I am, the "wife" I am called to be, the "mother" I am blessed to be, and the "witness" I am "ordained" to be. Everything else will fall into place. God will always take care of His own, and when sin enters the camp, you are sinning against God, and He can and will hold us accountable in more ways than we or anyone "earthly" can.

CHAPTER 21

"U" UNITE

THERE IS STRENGTH IN numbers! Have you heard that before? I'm sure you have. So, since you have, why is it so hard for people to unite? Pride and selfish desires are the main culprits. Interestingly enough, ants are aware of the benefits associated with uniting. We were created to unite! If we study the many definitions associated with unite, we will notice a common denominator ... "reconcile," "bring together," and "common purpose." Note the Book of Matthew 3:24: "... first be reconciled to your brother ..." vs 25: "Come to terms quickly with your accuser." Uniting is a requirement for healthy progression; however, uniting people means meeting them where they are. This is what we, as counselors, are trained to do. We meet people where they are. We don't and you shouldn't judge a person for being where they are; you simply get into the space of where they are and relate to them from that point. You will never know what it's like in someone else's shoes, even if you have similar stories. Taking the judgment away and embracing where they are at that given time is the prerequisite for unity.

Another way to begin the uniting process is to respect that wherever they are is where they are at that moment, and that moment only. The key to uniting is Matthew 18:20: "For where two or three are gathered in my name, there I am among them"... that's unity. Being on one accord requires humility and sacrifice of self. We are innately selfish, but we do not have to be self-centered.

CHAPTER 22

"V" VICTORY

VICTORY IS DEFINED as success in dealing with the enemy! Growing up in Shreveport, Louisiana, my home church, St. Peter Baptist Church, had annual choir musicals. "Back down memory lane!" Our ministers of music, the late David Taylor and the late Rickey Houston (my cousin), taught us one (1) particular song that still rings in my spirit! Albert Lattier would be on the piano, Rhoda Hayes would be on the organ and/or singing, and Roman Banks (first childhood crush and now Southern University Head Basketball Coach) would be on the drums! There's a song entitled "Victory Shall Be Mine", which was written by the late Rev. James Cleveland. The words are, "If I hold my peace, let the Lord fights my battles, I know that the Victory shall be mine, victory shall be mine!" Those are some powerful words. It is amazing how, as a child, I sang songs but did not truly understand the meaning. As an adult, I know exactly what each and every song I sang back then means today. Thank you Lord for the divine revelation of 1 Corinthians 12:11: "When I was a child, I spoke like a child, I thought like a child, I reasoned like a child. When I became an adult, I gave up childish ways." As a child, the "music" sounded good and had great Southern Baptist "rhythm," but as an adult ... "NOW" the words heal my soul, calm my fears ... they give me (and will give you) peace and ultimately victory.

There are times when we find ourselves in situations and we know that we are right, but we just have to sit back and/or step back, and kneel down to pray. This is not "always" an easy task, but it is something we all must do—that is if we want the victory. 1 John 5:4 makes it plain: "For everyone who has been born of God overcomes the world. And this is the victory that has overcome the world—our faith." The situation may look dim and your resources may be exhausted, but it is when we are weak that our God is strong (2 Corinthians 12:9): "... My power is made perfect in weakness." Your testimony of endurance, faith, and victory cannot be made manifest unless God is in it. This is why the battle is the Lord's and He wins the battle. Now, God's win may not be considered a win to you! Win does not mean you won't endure trials; win does not mean that you won't experience the same or similar situations as non-believers; a win is not when someone who has wronged you suffers the consequences immediately. Remember Isaiah 55:9: "For as the heavens are higher than the earth, so are my ways higher than your ways and my thoughts than your thoughts." God handles each situation as He so chooses because it's His victory.

CHAPTER 23

"W" WEALTH

WEALTH IS THE ABUNDANCE of valuable resources! The key word here is abundance, which means a large quantity. Why is it that people are not content with what they have? Why is greed such a rising problem in this society? People today are determined to have more—cars, money, houses, clothes, and jewelry. Money is not evil; it's the love of money that causes problems. I met a very materialistic yet low self- esteemed woman who arrogantly stated, after having one (1) good job with benefits, that she'd never drive anything less than a Mercedes-Benz; granted she arrived in Texas driving an old, maintenance-deprived Camaro and experienced very humble beginnings in Alabama. It was soon after that self-uplifting statement that she was laid off from work (go figure). The layoff <u>did not </u>dilute her pride.

The thirst became real for her; as well as her competitiveness with other women (young and old). Her husband, who had already been laid off from work, ultimately decided (for the sake of peace) to cash in all of his savings and retirement because she took her wedding ring off (refusing to wear it ever again) stating that she wanted another one. Seriously?! Now a "friend" of mine once mentioned during casual coffee conversations (CCC) that "Old money whispers and New money yells." That is so true. "Old money" is a person who has <u>always had money</u> but remains quiet because it's their normal. "New money" is a person who has <u>never had money</u> and they want you to know they have it by being loud. This lady (not a friend, just a passerby) was yelling (and still is) at the top of her lungs. I've never seen such an unhappy woman in my entire life, all due to the desire for an abundance. Low self-esteem and insecurities will display themselves in the most peculiar ways. She has aged horribly and we (African-American women) tend to age gracefully.

There is nothing wrong or sinful with working hard or wanting nice things, but it shouldn't consume you. The Bible talks about this! Matthew 19:16–22:

"And behold, a man came up to Him saying, 'Teacher, what good deed must I do to have eternal life?' And He said to him, 'Why do you ask Me about what is good? There is only one who is good. If you would enter life, keep the commandments.' He said to Him, 'Which ones?' And Jesus said, 'You shall not murder, you shall not commit adultery, you shall not steal, you shall not bear false witness, honor your father and mother, and, you shall love your neighbor as yourself.' The young man said to Him, 'All these I have kept. What do I still lack?' Jesus said to him, 'If you would be perfect, go, sell what you possess and give to the poor, and you will have treasure in heaven; and come, follow Me.' When the young man heard this he went away sorrowful, for he had great possessions." SMH!

One thing is for certain—when you die, there is no U-Haul trailing your hearse. When you have things and those things have you ... you have a situation that does not fare well. Kirk Franklin sings a song titled "Silver and Gold." The words truly resonate with the above Bible passage and the above lady I've met, in passing, during my Texas tenure. Matthew 16:26: "What profits a man to gain the whole world but lose his soul?" Both individuals have a level of arrogance that surpasses all understanding, and their heaven is here on this earth. They have their reward—the rich man and the Southern "Bell." We should and can learn from the numerous examples provided in the Bible and through our mere acquaintances.

CHAPTER 24

"X" EXCEPTIONAL

EVERYTHING YOU DO SHOULD be "better than average." You are a child of the most high king; you are royalty! When God created you, He took His time and created you in His image. God knows exactly how many strands of hair and/or hair follicles are currently on your head! My pastor, Thomas Bessix, says quite often, "Excellence is the Standard." I hate to be the bearer of unpleasant revelations, but I must continue to inform you that just because you give "better than average" does not mean that you will get it back in return. You are never held responsible or accountable for what people say, do, or give you. Your work should always represent you, and if you are saved and a Christian, your walk, talk, and actions should represent He who you claim to follow, Jesus the Christ.

What does it mean to be better than average? Well, it means *walking away*, when you can *stay* and contribute to or win the argument; *praying*, when you can easily enhance the *gossip*; *abstaining from sex*, when you can so easily *yield* to the temptation of the flesh; *serving*, when you can so easily sit and *be served*; *worshipping*, when you can't see the end result of a prayer request when it's easier to *wait* for a sign; *telling the truth*, when a *lie is easier* and more convenient to tell; *being a doulos* (Greek for *bond servant*), when it's easier to serve in the church *pew ministry* (Bessix, 2016); and *tithing*, when it's easier to *shop* the Macy's One Day Sale! These are just a few suggestions of things to be "better than average" at. Your list will differ from others and that's OK. We all have different lives and different things that we should be "better than average" at.

CHAPTER 25

"Y" YOUTHFUL

ATTITUDE IS CONTAGIOUS, so choose whom you spend quality time with very carefully. Life happens and situations will drain you (if you let them), but you must find or create your own "*Fountain of Youth*"! Now, the *Fountain of Youth* is a spring of water that "supposedly" restores the youth of anyone who drinks or bathes in its waters. I have a simpler way of restoring youth:

"TAKE BACK YOUR LIFE FROM THE ENERGY DRAINERS!"

You can't look like, or act like, what you're going through or what you've been through. I've met people who I thought were "much older" than they actually were "only" to be later informed that they were "younger" than me. This happens when you allow the "Situations of Life" to set up permanent residence in your heart. Just as people often say, the "Eyes are the windows to your soul"; well, "What's in your heart is displayed in your actions." If your heart is weighed down with depression, condemnation, the lack of forgiveness, low self-worth, and no self-awareness ... trust me—you will age well before your time.

You have no control over all situations that you encounter, but you do have control over how you deal with them. You can either deal with them or allow them to deal with you. Not dealing with them will deplete you of your energy. When you have no energy, those things that you once enjoyed doing, you now no longer have the desire to do. The places you enjoyed going to, you now find no enjoyment in going.

Stress is an equal opportunity condition, and it will rob you of your youthfulness. Stress will cause you to lose sleep, which creates those unsightly brown circles around your eyes and/or red lines in your eyes—all due to fatigue. When you are experiencing fatigue, you are mean-spirited. If you don't believe me, ask an innocent bystander (family or friend) who feels your wrath when you haven't had a good night's sleep. Or take notice of a baby who is sleepy but doesn't want to go to sleep, or can't!

Worrying is also an energy-drainer and will rob you of your youthfulness. First, you must realize that worrying never changes a situation (Matthew 6:27). Once you come to this realization, ask yourself if the situation is solvable. If it is, begin healthy brainstorming in efforts to find resolve. If not, 1 Peter 5:7 encourages us to "Cast all of our worries upon Him, because He cares for us."

The main goal is not to allow anything to cause you to age faster than you are supposed to.

"Z" ZEALOUS

THE WORD THAT COMES to mind when I see or hear the word "zealous" is "devoted." What or who are you devoted to? The only one who has earned, who's worthy and deserving of your devotion (i.e., loyalty) is God. Why? Because He sent His son, Jesus the Christ, to die for your sins. Now, I know you are saying, "I'm devoted to my spouse" or "I'm devoted to my children." I hear ya, and those devotions are noble, but your devotion should be to the one who gives life and who gave you life, who instructs your heart to beat, your eyes to blink, your lungs to inhale and exhale, your blood to flow through your veins and to clot when there's a cut, the mind regulator, the healer, the forgiver, the author and finisher of your faith, the one who watches over you while you are asleep, who wakes you up every morning, who can speak to the winds and the waves and they listen and obey (Matthew 8: 23–27). No other man or woman on earth can do any of these things.

Some of you are devoted to your job and/or career. I understand this completely. However, the last time I checked, jobs come and go. You can have a job today and could possibly be laid off tomorrow (or even today). God, however, is omnipresent and has a great and proven staying record (Deuteronomy 31:6b). Others are devoted to their organizations. Well, in *these* organizations, others have a "say" in your membership—good standing, active, suspended, etc. With God, no one can put you out and no one can put you in. (Sidebar: isn't it a blessing to know that "NO ONE" has a heaven or hell to put you in! Thank you, Jesus!) With organizations, you can take a leave of absence or cancel your membership, upon their approval … (hence, a lot of power to give someone who has no power). But with God, salvation cannot be canceled; His son, Jesus the Christ, died and rose. That's it and that's all. Now, "You", on the other hand, may take a leave of absence (Luke 15: 11–32; the story of the Prodigal Son). But even that particular son knew when it was time to come back home, and he did, and his father was standing there "looking and waiting" for him. And when he saw him from afar, he ran to him and drew him in.

God is the same way (Luke 15: 1–7, the Parable of the Lost Sheep). Are you that one sheep that has strayed away, wandering off into "never-never" land? Are you that one sheep that has misplaced your devotion to God by devoting to something that only has social or worldly benefits? I spoke to a lady once who I refer to as an "over-the-top politician." She is not a politician, but she has politician tendencies (only concerned about herself and getting a vote). (Sidebar again: all politicians are not like that; I've met some phenomenal politicians who are the total opposite. Just wanted to clear that up before rumors and gossipers get started.) She told me how much she loved an organization and was devoted to it until the day she dies. OMGosh … now, this young lady (anyone I'm older than I refer to as "young lady") willingly places the organization above God, her husband, and her children. I had to remind her that when she is called home to glory and has to stand before God, the one with whom her devotion should rest, He is not going to ask her about her organization, position in the organization, photo opportunities, speaking engagements that benefited her and only her, etc. God is not going to ask <u>any of us</u> about these earthly organizations. (Review Matthew 19: 16–22.) I was disappointed by her answer for the sake of her soul, but I was not surprised by her answer. When I see her all over social media, the song by CeCe Winans rings in my ears, "Not on His Knees Yet," and I pray for her.

I encourage everyone who's reading this book to read Matthew 6:33, "... seek <u>first</u> His Kingdom and His righteousness..." and allow that scripture to take precedence in your heart and mind. That's the proven way to survive "*Life Situations*"!